ZEN CYMRU

for Sue

Peter Finch

ZEN CYMRU

SEREN

Seren is the book imprint of
Poetry Wales Press Ltd.
57 Nolton Street, Bridgend, Wales, CF31 3AE
www.seren-books.com

ISBN: 978-1-85411-500-3

A CIP record for this title is available from the British Library.

The publisher acknowledges the financial assistance of the Welsh Books Council.

Front cover photograph by David Hurn.
Back cover photograph by John Briggs.

Printed in Bembo by Thomson Litho, Glasgow.

Author's website: www.peterfinch.co.uk

Contents

Up To A Certain Age You Have To Collect Them

The mothers stand around the school gates
in their jumble clothes and jumpy boots.
Their children are like a squall of fresh leaves
flying fingers out.
The mothers lift on scuffed toes
The children run on stalks.

The children shout around the school gates
their blue shirts flapping like flags.
The mothers are breathless step-aerobic
opening their arms.
The children are like a bath-water whirl
flecked with badges and bags and hurled-on coats.

The mothers are anxious like offtune radio.
Their children are soft like Azores wind.
Their noise you cannot you can you can't,
tear-gas, smell of milk and sweet sweat, thick.
This life flickers for a time, smiling,
and they want it to, then suddenly it's gone.

After The Row

He borrows her blue scarf she doesn't know about this.
He runs out into the night of ginkgo and frost.
He is four times around the park   his breath is smoking
his bones like glass rods.
He is frozen to the cracked path and dead.
He is in the deep woods lost.
He is crying into his hands.
He is small so small but not invisible.
He is smashing the street ice by stamping
People would look but there's no one there.
His head is lit red and his breath is burning.
He is flailing his arms nothing works.
He has checked everything and still does not understand.
How could she?
The wind comes in from the east full of knives.
He winds the scarf around him
her sweet smell for a moment
and then it's gone.

Section D

She couldn't remember him properly
anymore   such a long time ago   she said
his photo on the wall in his army uniform
his dark Italian hair
in the garden the leylandi were taller
than I'd ever seen them
fury in their tops   his tree-cutters
rusted in the shed.   In the
cemetery section D with the rain
sluicing down the ground's sliding surface
I can't find the stone can't remember
the date. I call him up but can't get
his voice right. It's like just
another recorded service call later
but do call. The past is huge I
flail in its mud. Can't go on like
this. I drive home and in the
washed silence where the storm
doesn't reach find his heart
still beating inside my chest.

Dorset Coast Path

east of golden cap there are
burned wooden leaves among
the cow pats and a stone acorn
litchening on the cliff top the
fence posts have gates hung by
binder-twine   arte povera in the
pressing sun   from the woods
on the path to nowhere step a
couple her white dress marked
with earth his cigarette trailing
slow smoke in the listless air
is it far he asks   it goes on
forever I tell him   I watch her
breasts from under the cotton
point the way   thanks mate
he says

Coming Back with JT and Bob Dylan

Returning to Wales on the train. They used to call it the 125 but they don't do that now.

There is downpour, always.
Fat rain hung over South Wales
like a diseased lung.
"There's many here among us
who think that life is but a joke."
Dylan, walkman, chrome band
of earphones across my head,
like a scar. Drove a shunter
once at Severn Tunnel. All the yards
now flat. Church with its spire,
stranger pointing a swollen finger.
Yellow rape bright in the rain,
land gouged by road and drain.

Tripp returning from foreign England
40 years back wanted border guards
to keep the place the same. But the terraces fail
and the tracks are crapped over with pitchmastic.
Jesus Saves – The Fuck He Does – white slapped
on a bridge side. Industry made hardcore
for car park.   Half of Wales with a
chipboard wardrobe, still overweight,
still dying of wet heart attack.
"They stone you when you're fit and able."
Two beers with JT's ghost in the swaying bar
full of men in bad suits who
sell and never go home.
Intellect and dignity buried.
The land leveed with golf, junk and garbage.
And God somewhere   making it worse.

Zen Cymru

Abereiddy !
Ah, Abereiddy, ah !
Abereiddy, ah !

The beginning of autumn
Sea and sea and sea
All the same

eeeeeeee eeeeeee
eeeeeeee eeeeeeee
eee eeeeees

ssss ssssssssss
sssss sss ssssss
sss sssssssee

Could be moon
Out there
Who cares

No more thunder
Hear hard belching
Outside the pub

By a cottage collapsed
Are men
Thinking of money

These sheep
So happy
How do you know they are not?

The stars speak so loud
In the Preseli blackness
It's just rain

Light over Trefdraeth
Behind the clouds
Then clear

The days go cold
And I am still in my khaki
Peg pants

This Wales leaks there isn't one
That doesn't
Is there?

Splottlands !
Ah Splottlands, ah !
Ah, Splott !

Tree looks like wind
Wave is moon spirit
Wrecked car what we do

On the great gable porch of
St John the Baptist Sikh glory
The butterfly bush still blooms

In this vast Wales you must not help yourself to any
meadow, flower or rockoutcrop that belongs to another.
Mountains, springs, the peat wildernesses all have an owner;
be careful about this.

Go out and you meet yourself
Come home
And you're still there

Is that the cloud moving?
Maybe
So what

On the headland
Do not speak
This is such a virtue

R S was once asked by an acolyte
"What is the meaning of the thin tongue inheriting
the universe?"
R S answered
"The mangels in the fields below the hills"

If you know, you don't speak
If you babble, you have no idea
We are a nation of noisy bastards

The sea darkens
You can see the small boats dumping oil drums
By the light of the stars

Sea
Ahh eeeeee
Ahh eeeeee

Saunders wrote, he could have done:
poems and science are opposed,
the former purposing immediate pleasure, unlike the
latter which is a hunt for truth.

Red face
In the endless field
Then back to the tractor

Going to Paradise is good, and to fall into Hell also is a
matter of congratulation. Old Buddha by the Golden
Road in the rocks of Foel Drygarn. Still invisible.

The ships pass but make no move to leave their reflection,
the sea makes no effort to hold how they look.
The clouds drift
it is spring, it is autumn.

They are young people. Though they are not
drunk they still wreck the station and
are sick before the passengers.

"But what am I to do?" said Alice. "Anything you like."
said the footman, and began whistling.

We hear the tune, you and I,
but inside our ears it is always a different one.

Rain

for my mother

How can I tell you about this? Me, always
full of what I am doing. I've been thirty years
trying to record how my pain can be ice rain
without knowing a thing about what pain really is.
Now, for you, the walls of the river are all that's left.
The rushing waters drive before them what was,
the past is worn to a veil of love and dust. Imagine this:
the mind giving up, saying that's it, dissolving
as you watch, all of you swept away by the rush.
Time does this, the bastard clock, the drip that wears the
stone, the feet that shape the steps. Your old self
smiles at me through collapsing mud.

We walk in the garden where the plants no
longer have names and the birds are blurs.
You are holding onto me with that clutch of
yours that crushes bones. Who are we,
mother and son in a rain which keeps getting colder?
The mouth won't answer, it doesn't know,
but the body, that remembers.

The Bosoms You Have Brought From Outside

We have taken out the contents of the
mini bar and are considering replacing it
with replicas from the supermarket
at a quarter the price. I have downed
more gin lying on the bed with the
air con thudding than I would in
a year anywhere else. We are ignoring
the sign on the back of the door that
tells us *The Food Or Drink That*
You Brought From Outside Will
Unfortunately Be Collected
From The Rooms. I will hide mine
in my lockable suitcase. Yours
will masquerade as presents to take back
home. The world is swirling and
you have removed all your clothes. I
hold the bed edge. The bosoms you
have brought from outside are bouncing.
I am older now yet they are still exciting.
Unfortunately I am unable to move.

I Chew My Gum And Think Of Rifles

What we needed was a
great leader in a set of Castro fatigues
with a gun. He would have
stood on the balcony they'd have
erected hastily along the front of City Hall
and told us we were worth everything
in the world and the enemy,
rich with gum and nylons, could go to hell.
Imagine that.
Strutting up and down Queen Street in
our camouflage pants with the
crowds roaring. No planes, we
wouldn't have planes. Some rusty vans,
maybe. And a truck, with a whole
crowd of us, singing and dancing on the back.

But it was never like that. We got people who
hectored us, with their hands in the till
and some fake tongue in their mouths.
Not one of them ever wore uniform.

I chew my gum and think of rifles.

Then I recall that we are a peace loving people,
full of mothers and hope. If we'd had rifles back then
by now we would have given them up.

Hunting For The Man With Huge Ear Lobes

It's difficult discussing Buddhism over
whiskey. It makes you laugh.
When you reach the tenets which
concern eternal suffering it's hard.
I imagine my father here with me. I am
explaining reincarnation but he won't
have any of it. I am no returned wood louse,
he insists. The bottle on the table
between us is going down at a terrific rate.

We aren't anything, says my father,
any of us, and when we go it's just
dark, you can't figure it, can you?
He's drunk, my father,
he waves his hands, this is how it is.

My father tells me alcohol is best consumed
lying down. Less chance of hurting
the living. We try this. His face still has that
lopsided look it had when I last saw him
flat-out in the morgue.

He is the greater vehicle, I am the lesser.
We drive on in the darkness looking for a
smiling man with huge ear lobes. He'll
have the answer, I say. No, says my father,
breathing softly. No he won't.

Watering Can

Some of us decide to have a fire to
add a little drama to the world. We fix it for a
bright boy from out of town to torch his
car outside the rear fence and set the study
roof on fire. The flames are great slashing
sheets. They do not douse when I drizzle
them with my green watering can. The
oily smoke has turned the world dark.
When the brigade arrive at last I am dancing
on the hot flat roof in my slippers
trying to stem the spread with a washing up
bowl and a mop. As the mask-clad firemen
spray everything with post-modern foam
their uniformed boss catches me to discuss his
novel. I'm having trouble with the plot,
he complains, steam and smoke pushing
past his head in streams. I find myself
advising on dialogue and offering to
re-enter the inferno to find him my copy of
101 Copyright Free Plots but the item is
burned to dust. When the party's done
and the police have left me a crime number
for the insurance I go to bed but do not
sleep. In the lane the car's skeleton clinks with
the night's coldness and the charred house timbers
flake in the wind. At the station the leading
fireman again battles with his novel. Amid the
smell of burning the most I can manage is a gob
of verse. This is it.

The Miró Mini Bar

Barcelona

By the lift-shaft we find a plaque
telling us that Joan Miró was born
in the very room in which we are
staying   seems so ordinary with its
minibar and shower-tray and Miró damp
marks moving up the wall. On the
street we see him standing outside the shop
which sells figs. I thought he was
dead but he's in fine form testing the
splatter technique he's learned from the
Americans on the front of the tapas bar on the
other side of the street. Free Political
Prisoners read the smears in red and
when the Guardia arrive to take him off
no one appears surprised that the country's
greatest painter should be treated like
this. Later in the bar a man with a moustache
tells me that was not Miró but an impostor.
"Miró, he never use words, too precise."
In the park his mute statue of giant woman
with bird glows in the sunlight. At the
hotel I take a beer from the Miró minibar
and consider its beauty. It has much –
slender, upright, radical. I check the
price. Large, traditional.
What would Miró have done?
In my notebook I do a little sketch of
the bottle. Then I put it back.

Foul Drainage

check fall of closet drain
insufficient at 12 meters
object intrusion
18% occlusion
recommend excavation carpet
underlay hard finish sub-floor
foundation dust hammer radio
with P16 battery strapped to outer-casing
using insulation tape eight hundred
plus tax decide to shit
in the woods

Real

I had these threads which went
out of me and connected with all the real
things in this world. I had no idea what
or where these were, I just needed
to stay joined up.
It was important, I felt,
to have something out there
I could believe in, just in case.
Lots of people do this –
Last minute conversions, bedside baptisms.
In Israel they circumcise the
converted dead as Abrahamic insurance.
Just before she died my mother went back to god
in a rush of repentance – held Jesus' hand –
hallelujah – did it help, we don't know.

Then I woke back up in the room with the
clatter of nurses and their sparkling eyes.

Threads gone, nothing came down them,
led nowhere, not this time.
No tunnels, no white lights.
All the ghosts of those I knew,
I never saw them.

The nurses give me water and
wheel me off through the fog,
my heavy bones still in touch.

The Runner

To make myself younger I run.
The gun metal sky soaks me so my chest
heaves through my t-shirt and my glasses
mist over so I see nothing
except their rims.

I lope along the brook near the quiet street
where I once lived, where the slick
of dumped sump slips through the reeds and
the locked park toilets cower quietly
their entrance lamps smashed to
smithereens.

For a moment the grass turns me sixteen
and I feel the sap engulfing my body
like a wet dream. I'm outrunning dogs,
yes, but they reach me,
snapping my heels, in the end.

The road back is a numb bone with heat
at both ends. The rain in sheets like a
power shower. I'm half blind
and I'm breathing half-century rasps
yet the world is leaping.

I don't age while I'm moving. No flake
amid the sweat. The blood is bright
it remembers. The years only roar again
when I cease.

King

When Elvis died, August, 1977,
Cardiac arrhythmia in the night at Graceland
a heart-stop straining at stool
so mundane for the burger king
I was in Buffalo Records, The Hayes,
thick with vinyl junkies,
blood pumping high.
The announcement they made over the
top of Queen sounded like a
train delay. The bub settled
briefly to half-heard stun
then a spike-hair shouted old fart
something and the paleness filled with
roaring. Who needs kings in
the anarchy republic? They didn't.
Never Came Here,
headline in the local press.
Not Dead Really. Working.
Asda, Merthyr. Seen at the fishpond
in Porth. Changing tyres
in Roath. Selling hotdogs in Newport.
Rocking in the free world.
Bingo calling at Splott Mecca.
Moved to Canton. Likes the damp &
the architecture. Plays Bill Haley
through the night. Later, alligator.
Half the world now
have no idea who he is.
An old man in a white belt.
Used to be something, didn't he?
Mumbling.

N Wst Brdg

30902

erth nt a thng so brill
hes dul v soul pssng by
sght of mjstic tch
cty now wrs grmnts
of mrng bty :-) slnt bare
Shps twrs dms thtrs + chrchs
opn t flds + sky – ^v^v^
brite glttrng in nosmke air
nvr sun so butfl steep
n hs 1st splndr vlly rck or hll
nvr saw nvr flt clm so deep!!!
rvr flws at hs sweet wll (own):
Deer GD! vry hses seem slp | |
+ all tht BIG HRT lyng still!

Wynd Cliff

Wordsworth's untrammelled
wildness   romantic path up 365 steps
to the edge of the Wye's Wynd cliff
no waymarks   a wrecked cottage
where they once sold teas   an
unreadable notice shot to buggery
by preyless hunters   he went
up here with Coleridge exalted through
a pre-raphaelite wreck of moss and riven
rock   saw the sylvan river   wrote nothing
down   at the top the fields are flaked
with frost   couple in the distance
exercising an Alsatian   kestrel scratching
the silent sky   I take a leak in a mess
of bramble   spotted immediately by
a bold walker striding rucksacked
from the trees   the synchronicity of the
wilderness   we do not nod

Facing The Flowers

Outside the window
a battleship sky;
a cypress imagining
its bracts to be starshells,
a shower of needles like
grey rain. In this dark corner
My mother and I would
face the flowers, so
few in the tired soil, yet
she wouldn't know their names.

At the church the order of service
was a cyclostyled list which trembled
without me even holding it.
We prayed amid the wreathes
and the pastor spoke of how she'd
always dressed well, so neat,
but I knew that inside the coffin
all she had on was cotton wool padding
and a swaddling sheet.

At the wake I asked for a whiskey
but there was none. Someone gave me
a plate with half a pork pie and
six crisps. On the lawn relatives
drew Benson breaths among
the brilliant border blooms.

My mother thought heaven
to be a place where blossom did
not fade and speech did not
matter. Starlings would pass
in great swarms, imagining
their wings to be
their hearts. The sun
would stay up forever.
There would be no dust.

How hard it is, in that dark corner
for anything to grow. But they
do, just. Floret, stamen, umbel.
I'll get their names.
I'll look them up.

Index to the Grand Holiday Club Timeshare Sellers Handbook

Llywelyn Goch ap Meurig Hen At Speed

South heart like a birchtop woodsong
light and little proud ah
Lleucu heart broken
Merioneth
Machynlleth
Mawddwy

Deheubarth buggered

the barbs of longing the pain

You've been writing again, she said,
no it's just blisters on my fingertips,
and great caves in
the space inside me. Heart
thinks it's the soul. Full of birds.

Life has five plots:
rise to fame, fall from grace,
gain love, lose it
and death.

Voice

Her phone sounds like it's
ringing when I call but
its plug has been pulled,
undone, torn out.
I put my ghost voice in through the
letterbox, a long grey thing of pain,
please, it says, my voice like a swarm
of flies. In the distance
there's a freight rumbling. On
the road a couple pass entangled
like a dream. I stand back and use my huge
lungs to rattle the dark windows like
a shower of stones. A light
clicks next door and quick before I'm
seen a shame in my rage
she lets me in.

Flock

The behaviour of crowds is not dictated simply by a kind of averaging of its members' feelings. There is actually no sorting out of the piles of mental furniture and building the one that sells. The alley run fills us with breath. A crowd is numbers and collective power. A power that fills. The crowd is anonymous. See it steam up the main street. We are all roaring boys. We are shed of responsibility. We are not clung about with caution. We have our t-shirt arms. Our cans. Our hands. We started out as mother's sons but this is contagion, now, hypnotist hysteria. Feel yourself bellow. Feel the passion. You shout that great big crowd roar, ahhh. You know the one, big and bigger. Yours and unmistakable. Let's try some now – yuggaha yugggaha yugggaha hoi yuggha hoi. This is it. Run run running, bit of that. Flock formation. Stream and throw. Steam and smash. Marching metal. Who can stop you? You pull your breathe up all of you. Arms and thundering. Group cohesion glued tattoo no individual. All subjugated the crowd and the rolling, roar the steaming, and the hoi hoi yuggha yuggha hoi. Red corpuscles stream the body. Oxygen river flow. Termites taking out a six mile fence. Nest afire. Hive exploding. Yugggaha breath yuggha mind yugggaha running. Nothing stuck. Nothing caught. Yugggaha empty. You imagine this is the place to meet with god. Might as well be. This is us in glory. Did you know Buddha had six million souls? He ran too. Steamed yugggaha yugggaha Siddharta yugggaha Gautama. The hysterical bodhisattvas. The steaming sutras. The world as one. Yugggaha face yuggaha mind. Nothing is new under the sun. Except maybe the tattoo about Millwall.

Chelsea Hotel

Built in 1884 as one of New York's first co-op apartments.
Later converted to a hotel. Associated with more writers
and counterculture artists than there are bagels at Zabars.

Beyond the Flatiron looking like the
superstructure on an art deco liner,
on W 23rd Street, in the creasing heat,
dark New York, brick and iron,
in the range of ground zero, but unshaken.
The Chelsea Hotel, where Ginsberg sold
Fuck You in the foyer, Corso crashed
stoned and Kerouac, in check shirt,
wrote *On The Road*, one long paper
roll through the nite, jamming speed
down his throat. De Kooning paid
his rent with enormous paintings
and Dylan Thomas lost his bag.

There are plaques now beneath the
iron balconies. Two Japanese taking
photos. One with a Leonard Cohen lp under
his arm as if he might find the master still
here and get the label signed.

Little has changed other than America itself.
This land has forsaken counterculture for fear,
left the zen dream drift in a different ocean.
Wall Street blocked, guns outside the
Stock Exchange, armour at Liberty,
holy streets holy walls holy dust.
Angelheaded hipsters who once bared
their brains to Heaven
now see death in the starry dynamo,
evil on tenement roofs,
and demons under the El.
That bag Thomas lost
it's a device don't touch it'll kill.

On the walk to the East River where
the 4th will be lit with thirty minutes of skyflash
and starburst courtesy of Macy's and the Mayor
the cops stop me three times to search
my bag, check my jacket, see I'm okay, no
semtex in my shoes no dynamite strapped to my
thighs.

In the twilit mass, steaming along Roosevelt
the crowd swear endless allegiance,
sing the star-spangled, shout for victory,
sway in the dusk, sweating and certain.
The fireworks in all their brilliance
can only support them.

Dreams! omens! hallucinations!
miracles! ecstasies! Gone now
down the American river!

1600 Degrees

I'd said I wouldn't rot, wouldn't crease,
wouldn't leak, become a slow sack
blistering with dysfunction. My firm
face would know all futures. I would
stop each slide by telling it. Tough it out.

My mother couldn't do this. Joints like
plumbing welds. Mind scoured thin
by time. My father with his morbid
aneurysm didn't get a chance. But I will.
Centrophenoxine, Vasopressin,
Levodopa, Vinpocetine, Phytomer, Botox,
Ginseng, Selinum, Roc, Ginkgo Biloba,
Phyllosan, Fish Innards, Bits of Trees,
Orange peel, Melatonin, Rubber Piping,
Cellex-C, Oil of Ulay Plenitude.
Stretching. Rubbing. Running.

But now I can see it. After five decades
among the women in white coats at
Boots. A sort of end but not an end.
The eyes that no longer penetrate,
the breath that doesn't last,
the arc that grounds, stops flying.

In the fire the skull goes last.
1600 degrees to sear it,
a crusher to turn it to white dust.
Mine will be full of Betaplex C.
It will roar like a roman candle.
Finch with his head on fire.

Didn't last. Doesn't matter.
Up there in the unblemished air
the arc becomes a shining circle.

Trying To Find Béla Bartók

Top of the hill at Farkasréti Temetö in a mild rainstorm.
The mamoushka flower sellers
in sailing polythene squat by the road.
A Trabant has its front off.
There are bullet holes in the ferro tram stop
and there's a man with a dog.
The guard at the car-park has
the red fire face of a drinker
and no knowledge of this land's greatest son.
The paths like death itself are interminable.
I find him next to Solti
marked by a chiselled bass clef
and overgrown with conifer.
There's a fragment of a red star
and no flowers.

Was your visit to Hungary: yes / no

Which of these: Concerto for Orchestra / Hungaroton /
Race With The Devil

Rate democracy: 1 - speech 2 - obstinacy 3 - epic
4 - fiction

How: tin can / mixer deck / mini-bar /
high-peak military cap (please circle)

Please hum 14 bagatelles into this microphone
köszönöm

Italian Masturbazione

The orgasm is one of the more intense pleasures that can be tried
even if of short duration. He seems natural to try to have of the greater
possible number through the sexual relationships or if can't with
the masturbazione. I even try to procurarsi the pleasure with
the masturbazione without to be involved with other persons.

I do not understand why one must limit when this is easy to obtain
and innocuous for the health. I do not eat manicaretti and leccornie
all days which in the long run can nuocere my health,
but I do try to have the greater number of orgasms
(also resorting to the masturbazione)
the pleasure that it gives to me is intense.

I am astonished that all are not behaved like me.
When then I feel the women that they consider the degrading
masturbazione and therefore to avoid, the arms fall off me.
Is there is something that does not go in this my way to think?

Spirit

When he found it the spirit was smaller
than it should have been. A bit like
the feed-bag they once used for horses
but woven from sparkly stuff
like you see when you press your eyes.

He picked it up shook it heard
the sound of oceans banging
the sound the past makes
when it gets upset.

It wouldn't fit anywhere
washing-basket bucket box
pocket suitcase cupboard shelf
sprawled from under the bed
like it was dead.

Then it began the humming,
an addled tune from Billy Cotton,
made him put a tie on sit up straight
stop fiddling shave. God this was no good.
Hadn't worn a suit since the funeral
years back. Didn't want to now.

Tried to cut the sparkly corner off
drain it into the shower get rid of it
but all the faces kept coming back.
Churchill Sooty Mr Hanlan Martin Towler
Mum Bill Halley Alan Breeze
Antony Eden Dad Terry Northmore
Danny Blanchflower Stanley Matthews
Stirling Moss Douglas Bader Dad.

Fixed it with Elastoplast like broken
glasses. Lumpy. Put it
under the tree. Lit up softly.
It was all ok after that.

Urology

hardly anything hurts here
front of the internet
finding out where it came from:

personal history,
recurrent urinary tract infection,
external beam radiation,
consumption of aristolochia fangchi,
infection by parasite,
caffeine, saccharin,
hairdresser, machinist,
printer, painter, trucker,
rubber, chemical, textile,
metal, leather worker,
smoker (greatest risk),
dark tobacco, after that light,
then second hand.
Caucasian,
male over fifty,
worse as you age.

Give up smoke. Get younger.

Have you brought your dressing gown? High eighties outside. I have not. You'd best wear this. Hospital tie-at-back shortie blue angel gown your NHS arse sticks out you can't go in there with your arse out I don't care put on these paper pants cover yourself there's a love. Cover my arse they won't. Edges flapping can't reach or be bothered. Goosebumps. Fear. You alright, Peter? You're next, my love. You are. There's a good boy.

On the screen it's like miniature DynoRod
hunting my house drains
water running so it slides
headlamp camera scouring plunger
At twenty meters they found a ring-seal loose
have to dig that out.

On the notes when I browse them
while the nurse is out
the sketch looks like a sea anemone
still life: bladder with flower
done in biro
sideways on the urine analysis
Red cells present: too
many to number.

My father died in this building
five floors up from where I am now
sunlight streaming through the glass
nurse with stockings clearly visible
under her white dress neither
he nor I bothering
him pulling hard for breath and me
holding tight his hand. End game.

But this time, not yet.
I put the gown in the dumper &
the pants in the bin.
Breathe again.

Entry of Christ Into Cardiff 2005

Anointed Christos Branch of Myrhh Jesse Jesu
Queen Street Elias Jeremias Ensign Immanuel Emmanuel
Jesus Multifloral Carfit Melchizedek Messiah
ObeWan Nazarene Kenobi Potentate Passover Owl
Rabboni Tortilla Bhoona Jasu Rose of Sharon Scepter
Isa Ibn Maryam al-Salaam Christ Shabazz Bandana
Yasu 'Isa bin Maryam Muslim Spire Eesa Esau Yeheshua
Rough Joshua Rahman Yoghurt Iēsous Abd of Allah
Jesus Cassanova Bute Street Sorrow Bethlehem
Llanrumney Passover Kalimatimmin Kalimaatullaah
Mary the Virgin Karate Do Splott Saviour Jesucristo come back
Kalimat'Allah (peace be upon him) Adamsdown Rasulullah
Jesu Prajapati Jehovah Lifeboat appeal Saturdays
Jesus latterday Cardiff Post Vishnu Ya Ruhullah
Enzikiriza Yaba'ddugavu Eye Nono Black Messiah
Saviour Turban Guru Gobind Singh Chapate handwrench
Blood of Ely glass and Potentate Refuge God Iesu
Diolchwch i Dduw y nefoedd Taff will baptise too late now
Bread of Heaven William Williams Cefn-y-Coed Llandovery
St Johns St Marys St Womanby fill slowly with beer

Clinic

The penis clinic in Victoriana prick todger prart pork sword skin flute throbber john thomas rusher old man glans proud slammer blaengroen carrot aardvark[1] hatband snozzle tickle-tackle whickerbill whistle full of glowing youth Sun Star Al-Jazirah Nike Nokia Nokia

Wash of at risk posters Tattooed Taken The Risk? Take The Test. Self Harm Don't Cope Alone. Missed Pill Oops. Injecting? Fight 4 Your Rights. HIV Find Out. Mobile Don't Use It. Everyone does.

How it goes here: fear, irrelevance, inconvenience, stuttering, ignorance, ineptitude, woke with zoon's bananitis, raging smegma, inflamed frenular veins, foreskin ballooning more likely secretion and vast redness pain when doing anything. This carn't be rite number M20446591 waiting in the floor-bolted lounge chairs like a battered airport departures. No air crew. Woman with a flowing white coat loose threads seen better days files under her arms circles. Pert African with tea mugs. Helper from Aberdare green bri-nylon who puts marks on forms. Janitor who ignores the flickering strip light. Delivery of boxes. Phone goes. No movement. Time settling like low fog. Battery gone from clock. Late arrival giant Rasta seen immediately. Continuum like a brick. Feet. Arms. Hands. Head.

Ages: 18, 18, 27, 32, 38, 17, 16, 57, 20, 21, 18, 16, 31, 20, 18, 27, 32, 38, 17, 20, 20, 20.

That many of us.

At the start of the 80s *Peeping Tom* poetry little mag put out a masturbation issue with work from Lee Starwood, Yann Lovelorn, John Squelch, Bill Sniffit, Barry McFuz, faded mimeograph foolscap photocopied porno shots pasted in and a cover made from wallpaper. Tristan Tzara save us – the rockets are thrusting. Opal L Nations. Bob Cobbing. Names like strata nimbus. Sex and Gestetner ink. 64-mil hard sized white stacked and circumcised.

I read the poems. Harwood's White Room. 60s. Feels like the past engaging with the present and failing. The light in here smears the words. Would have changed the world but the world shifted first.

1. told by the Dixie Chicks to English TV host Graham Norton.

At Urology reception next to Transplants it's like the 4am flight to Gran Canaria tshirts sunhats slop loud everything but no larger. They move you to a second waiting area to keep the stats in shape. One side of me a seventy-year old on a wheeled walking frame, trouble talking doesn't stop him reading out extracts from the *Daily Mail*. Woman found the face of Christ in a Sesame Ryvita. White hat like a cricket umpire. To my right eighty five, shouts it, won't drink enough water to pee can't be seen until he can drink this don't want to must.

You have names here. Mr Jones. Three of them. Mr Williams. Four of those. Mr Finch. He's three hours down the list.

Here Harwood fits. A soft pearly brightness in the mist. Lines twisting between shuffle and cough.

The walls warn me against smoking, advise me on bedwetting, tell me not to be frightened when parts of me leak, lisp, leer, illuminate, inflate, conflate, flag, fail, flounder, finish. They show me how to complain, inform me of support groups, let me lean amid their upbeat public service chatter. Leechate is feared in landfill. Here it simply seeps across the floor.

In the lane I've put six boxes of old little mags. *Tlaloc. Ambit. Mainly. Element. Rumpus. Oasis.* The staples rust. Damp grows on the lower pages. They fold and fade. Mould and foxing. White encrustation. Skin blemish unmoveable by cream. The poems had poor life then, none now. Most of them. Many about self. A few about love. None of them about urine. Transmissions of hope gone into dust. There are some of Mottram's *Poetry Review*. Best of the period a radiance. I yank them back. Most of this detritus, though, won't even burn if I lit it.

There's a photo in there too. Bunch of poets gathered to celebrate the small printing of something. Reid wearing a sombrero, J Tripp with a pint in his hand. Cobbing smiling. Bob Thomas happy just to be in front of the lens. All dead. Me, who held the camera, the only survivor.

Bloods. Wait. Biopsy. Wait. Check with light on a stick. I practise breath patterns. On the out breath how many words can I string? More than Ginsberg. Worth writing down? No.

This cure anti-viral. Side-effects: lights, nausea, skin rash (occasional), rush of creativity. Shortness of breath. Insight. Ability to manipulate paragraphs. Good recall. Remove staples.

Fix the past by deleting the cache.

Wide

His arms are wide and he speaks to me
but I cannot hear.

It's been seventeen years but the reality
doesn't change.

He's telling me that it's okay   like he
always did   need this now just
as much as then.

He looks the same too   years spent
counting the cars that go by
the graveyard   what else is there to do?

I want to ask him a lifetime of things
didn't then   now there's this sheen of
mist   mouth is empty.
He's pale   but he's real   it's him.

I tell my head to shut up
stop these magic pictures   flaring   roaring.
Blink and blink   but he doesn't vanish
arms stay imploring.

He still has on those thick rimmed glasses
helping him see doesn't need them now surely?

Sight of them again clutches my throat
I run upstairs and check the box   still
there   and his hat   dust of decades   those
gone and those coming.

Is this it, I mouth at him.
but he's not answering.

My Mother's Doors

There were twelve of these
spread across the city,
most of them still green or
cream even after fifty years.
Places we'd lived in for a decade,
or only for days, as my
father bought and sold, making little more
each time than it cost to load our stuff
and drive. The Romany gene.
His father's origins were wiped from the
record. The one trace left,
in an army paybook, had been inked
out by my mother, who hated where
anyone was from that wasn't here,
in this, the latest house, with its
Edwardian leaded lights around
its Cardiff door.

I photographed them, these gates
to the past, houses spurned.
I collected a set and showed her,
face drawn, hair unpermed,
at the place where you go when your mind
gets worn thin by the roll of time.
She recognised nothing. Uncertainly smiled.

Green, she said, eventually.
Of that she was sure.

Looking For The Southern Cross

Looking for the Southern Cross wasn't easy
Lonli our guide, a Jehovahs, said god was in
all things including Bulawayo but he had
no idea. Try town. Natural History Museum full of
tired lions but no planetarium. The guard said cross
boy you want Jesus. Maybe I did. In the Alabama Club
where Wistom Bhunda and Smiling Sliders hammed it with
red and blue shirted jive dancers showing teeth like
diamonds no one knew. In the sky I counted three crosses
god on southern overdrive. Outside the bottlestore the touts
and layabouts wore crucifixes. Old habit.
Robert Moffat started all this coming here from Ormiston
in 1859 with a bag of bibles. There's
a faded shot of him and his wife somewhere looking
like mill workers about to become holy sunbeams. Southern Cross
pulled him. Hard. He gave the Ndebele ground nuts, Jesus
and workless Sundays. God's done them proud.
The night sky is huge and unmasked
full of milky clusters of unpolluted light.
Beyond the centre the townships shake and suffer
no god, no planning, homeless under the bastard cross,
chased by a minotaur with no civilization.
Moffat bring back your singing. On the streets
they don't. The Southern Cross is up there by
the Coalsack but no one looks.

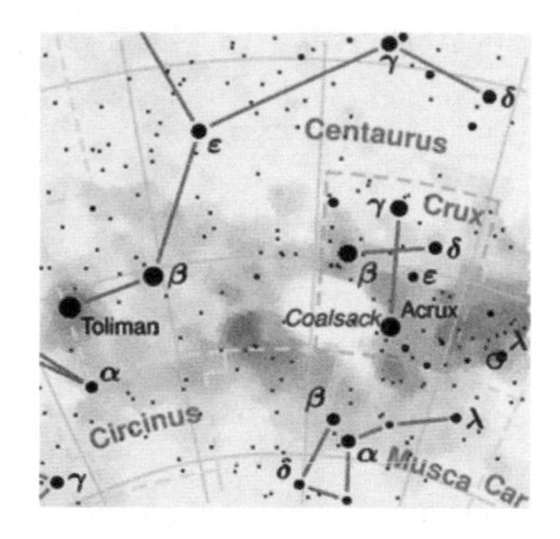

Sport

After 11am on Saturday
sport took over the world.
Followers' brains
softened as they leaned into
blether about the fitness of players
and the women of managers and the
sliding of endless goals on
swathes of green across the land.
This was all so important, you understand,
more than politics or science or love
which had become addling messes
that would stop drink from entering
your veins if you let them. Sport
was king, a thing we could all afford
24/7 no need for earning
or buying boots or washing
the dirt from soft faces
western money comes free
just ask and you get.

The goals went in like needles
feeding our need none of us
moving far from anywhere
full of lager like urinals. There's
a god out there so what we know more
than he does. Reruns of everything
these kitted men do from every angle,
don't worry if you blink your eyes.

Mirror

Looking in the mirror
in my suit
at how it was and how
it is.
My son behind me
seeing how it
will be.   Soon.

He's bought a house
with leaking pipes
and rot enough
to turn him expert
in the way things are.

They always depreciate
more than they gain, things. Failure
gets fixed fails again.

He'd take up my carpets and
laminate the floors, he says
change the colours
fix the things I fixed
do it all once more.

Spend a little on a suit
and get the legs ironed slim.

Buy a mirror of his own
to watch the future repeat
with all its fluent magic
those things it insists
cannot change.

Chance

with random realistic (Schwitters,
Chopin Mac Low) the
desire (deep) (dear) (double)
(diff) to interfere (amend) infer
can prove hard to
resist (wrist) (flex) (fix) (shuffle hand)

generators can do and do   do   streams
and sheets (ream)   who
might read them?   listen
(easier) (have to) (sleep)
working out like you expected? no/no*

**delete one.* done this before.[1]
(*Form.* Poems For Ghosts)

types of:

divination
sequencing
bibliomancy
probability theory
types of force
random generator
Brownian motion
entropy

the number is cursed
the number is due
both (failures) fallacies

take the dice (throw)

1. see also p38 this vol. Another tack.

The Death of Phil Ochs

Vietnam at its peak Ochs reached Cardiff
played the old red-brick student's union
before they pulled it down.
A church full of slim-jeaned hipsters
polo-necked   beards.
It was their war not our war the
bombs of others their blood their fire.
Tet and Mai Lai and Nixon's
peace with honor a thousand miles away.
Didn't stop us wanting our protesting heard.
Ochs came on to cheering I Ain't
Marching This is the Land of The Power and
the Glory Did The Bells and The Highwayman twice
had us on our feet did once more.
Life in his eyes like electricity
the demons of doubt and
the fear of failure yet to burn.
Took six more years until
the war was over and the bipolar raging
ran in his veins enough to wreck him.
Hung himself at his sister's home
in Far Rockaway NY. Lamé suit in
the case. No gold records on the wall.

Out in the street after the union gig. By the train tracks.
Lines to the coal. Ochs his hands in his pockets. On his own.
Went for a curry. God what a south Wales thing.
Talked about guitar chords and Minnesota
and his friend his not friend Bob
and a bit about lithium and the way the sun always rose.
Didn't mention pain or death. Next gig somewhere north
of here. Just a walk up the road. Didn't mention
death at all.

Ikea

A visit to the Cardiff Grangetown branch
bright yellow and blue amid the red brick terraces.

A Shanghai manager reports that
23 families daily (av) use his
store for picnic   provide own foodstuff
use store utensil   Arv cutlery
Snudda serviettes   Parad plates.
We are above all this.
Here where the gas works once stood
in our yellow-blue hanger
branded *Go Wild With Textiles*
we are lost among the Aars self-assembly TV stands
and Hemorod beds with foot-locker and arm rest.
We watch what was once the working class
sashay past dressed by Matalan and Cotton Trader.
The tattoos on their backs replicated on Ikea's
cushion covers and Griprip fabric throws.
Six developing world aspirational Marlboro smokers
wheel an ash veneer Poofsvåk corner wardrobe
towards check out. Recommended assembly time
thirty minutes actual assembly time two days.
They sleep in it when done. Here
the world runs in prime time, fills itself with
Lingonberry tunishafish and biscuits made
from cardboard and wall insulation. Free
pencils. Incomprehensible Nigerian
tannoy announcements. Surcharge if you
want to use plastic. Amid the Bimbum shelves
I relax on a Pondorosa armchair and browse one
of Ikea's hundred and eighty demonstration copies of
Upptäck Natuerens Hemsteadligheter
photos of fish in Swedish wildernesses
just how it is.

R. S. Visits The City

R. S. Thomas – born Cardiff 1913, died 2000

This city is now spinning like an exhibition
for cities. Clear and clean. Full of aspiration
and landmark work. Sort of rocks.
Yeats never came. Pound did not.
Nor Eliot. What did they want with
drizzle and dirt? R.S. Thomas was different.
A thin faced return in his reverend's suit. Sat
before the snaking queues in the Royal Hotel
siarad am pwrpas, siarad am ysbryd, siarad am iaith,
signing effortlessly his enormous books.

This was the man who'd come to the city
before, years ago, hating it, sitting for thirty minutes
unmoving on stage, not a flicker, even of
his eyes, then slowly undoing his
string-tied bundle of printed matter to read
without interruption or explanation or
even the slightest elevation of the voice
his existential patriotic verse   letting
it swirl into the vortex of our ears. At this 30 year
distance I can't recall
anything of the content only that it
shimmered like dancing motes.
The poet now is himself dust
and the people who knew him faltering. The
venerated verse lowering like an aging beast
inside his reprinted books.

In his work are there traces of this place,
where he was born, reluctant, leaving
as fast as he could? Do the streets of Cardiff echo?
No, they don't. Do we honour him in this
city as a lost son? Plaque, statue, trail?
No we do not.

Not Welsh enough, us, for a man redolent of
rural fields and revolutionary fire.
In Wales cities are alien places.
I had a postcard of him printed, black
and white, shot of a younger man, smiling. I'd destroy
those if I were you, he advised, when I showed
him. Went out the shop door to walk among
Bute's trees in the great park where the air was clean
like it was in Llŷn. And after he'd returned to
his stone cottage where the past burned
but the heating didn't work I put the cards on full display.
Sold the lot.

Kerdif

Dŵr Caerdydd mate
pal aright skip
Cocks Tower Tŵr
bibles henges fish
imprisoned recidivist Rawlins
right White matey mate

Milkmaid Hayes Waterloo Bridge
Glam canal
ditch and flumen
Taf floodplain flud
pont point pint port pwynt

Sabrina Afon Hafren
Severn solid
Sandy Roman frith

Kerdif Cairdiffe

quid est?
beth yw hwn?
what is this?

Greyhound Spice Box antiquarian
Huxley's surgical goods
embiggened bog shoreline sunk
alluvial gravel buried books
wall and garden   canal ley

Russell Dunleavy Jack Brooks
Bute Wood Hugh Despenser
John Batchelor Llywelyn Bren
Shirl Vic Billy Dannie Frank
Gilbert de Clare John Cory Mary Clark
Tosh Billy Raybould Terry Nation

Thrasher Box Stockdale Superted
Jim Driscoll Mike Harries Peg-the-Wash
Billy-my-Stick Hairy Mick
Cochfarf Dammy Sammy
Bin-banger Ninjah Toy Mic Trevor

Psychic centre south Cardiff
y man lle mae'r pŵer yn cwrdd
place where the power seeps

Near this spot you could once
cross a Cardiff bridge
before that a Norman ditch
then Welsh water
then Roman mud

Was there much here
found in the clay?
socketed axe head
with converging ribs
bone fragment pot
a few microliths

Now all lost

Colin Baker Dr Who
1986 time capsule
didn't find this

Future future
Llên Caerdydd Cardiff shine
Cardiff books Empty Caerdydd bricks

Ca yr d i f

G a e R dy dp I AE

K E R D I F V

C a Ke r d i f DI

ar i K E R D Y F AR

di rd yf K p r e a C

ff i aird

e f iF dif r ai K

The Ballast Bank

Amharic
Afghan
Algebraic
Anthracite
Angelic
Alexandrian
Albanian
Arabeg
Abyssinian
Baptist
Bangladeshi
Basque
Bengali
Benaadir
Birmingian
British
Bituminous
Butelike
Bulgar
Breton
Cambrian
Caribbean
Castilian
Cornwallian
Cape Verdean
Cardiffian
Cantonese
Cornucopian
Cymraeg
Creole
Cymric
Cyrillic
Cypriot
Danish
Docker
Dean Forester
Egyptian
Efengylaidd
Galeg
Gogleddian
Greek
Gujarati
Hebraeg
Heddgeidwaid
Heddychwyr
Heddforwyn
Hindavi
Hispanic
Ironic
Indian
Irish
Italian
Jodhpur
Jew
Arabic Juba
Klingon
Korean
Kurdish
Lithuanian
Latino
Mandarin
Mirpur Panjabi
Maltese
Mormon
Maay
Môn
Midlander
Native
Nobiin
Naval
Northumbrian
Norman
Northwalian
Orthodox
Norweigian
Potato
Raiders (Viking)
Russkii
Rhondda
Rich
Roman
Sikh
Saesneg
Steel
Sinhala
Swedish
Swazi
Af Soomaali
Sindhi
Sailing
Sylheti
Stockdalian
Sicilian
Texan
Tamil
Tagalog
Tongwynlais
Tonpentre
Tonyrefail
Tonypandy
Turkish
Toaster
Tiger Growling
Ukrayins'ka Mova
Vlax Romani
Victorious
Vulcan
Urdu
Venusian
Yiddishe
Yoruba
Yemeni
Farsi (East)
Farsi (West)

Eritrean
Estonian
Elemental
Evangelical
Frank
Filipino
Fishermen
Farsi
Glamorgan
Georgian

Germanic
Portuguesa
Petroleum
Polski
Quick
So Quick
Qashqai
Road
Rail
Redlight

Boat Barge
Rat Islander
Welsh
Welsh
Ysgotyn
Ysbaenwr
Hope
Light
Croeso
Welcome

Technique Comes Hard

Technique comes hard. Staying the course. Doing things once. Doing them again. Alcohol eases. Nuttall said you can avoid all these issues by staying high. Ah the blur and the power and the out of focus fuzz. We were in the bar and should have been on stage. Nuttall's stage. Lunge at the microphone like a maypoll. Wet mouth like MacSweeney open mouth like Zukofsky hard mouth like Hausmann Welsh mouth like RST. Poem bug pom pim. Got this got this. Paper papur doesn't matter. Spit. Shower. Hold on hold on. This sentence has an end.

Nuttall said slow hell slow they want you to read poems give em a novel give them fiction stream of consciousness can't tell the beginning from the end. Like Warhol's Empire State was it the Empire State culture of the bomb all they want is to know that time's gone by. New stuff sod new stuff they don't want that. They ask these old blues harp revivalist guitar pickers found on stoops out in the back of dust southern states well what was it like in 1936 in that studio shack south of the tracks when you were on form and who played behind you was it Shaking Hard Arm or Blind Blake on bass? Guy doesn't know can't recall all he wants to hear is how it is today on what he's just laid down. Those twelve bars has he still got it? Tell me man tell me. Willie McTell could have done that better. Son House, Lightning, Sleepy John.

Met X at the bus station driven here from iron Germany welcome to the drizzle still old world but light in the skies. Haversack full of pubs. These for review put them in the mag. *Second Aeon* that was once part of my life. These are boxes that held 7" reels of Scotch magnetic tape. One full of shaving foam and an oily bolt. One cutupbits unspliced rattles. One little mimeo products and a book of matches. One with battery and balloon (uninflated). One with sweet wrappers some ink cake mix and a Bible page. Threads watch dial. Parts of loaf immersed in paint. Vinyl holding shape like landscape of the Herefordshire fields. Recalls Nuttall. I say this. I am ignored.

We stack them. Ideas. Put them in a bucket to get echo. Get the drums from tapping the side of the booth and the edge of the chair. Flared trousers. Big haircuts. Oxfam jackets. Drink takes the edge. Somewhere it always comes together. Jeff told me that.

In the new world the past is invisible. Nuttall vanished. His poems impossible to get. The view is a year long only. No one looks further back than that. Discover what's already been discovered. Invent again what's been invented. Say you are new. Wave a flag. Tell them. Then tell them once more. Then tell them you've told them. Nothing much matters after that.

The Trial of Phil Spector

There's a wall of guns.
Spector puts one to the dark head of
Leonard Cohen. Fires one at Lennon while
making Rock'n'roll. Another at Dee Ramone
when he won't play bass. Waves one at Ronnie when
she says she's going. Shows her a gold coffin in the basement.
Glass lid. Says you'll be in that if you
so much as speak to anyone,
you infidelious slap.

Says mild mania relatively insane prescription drug overdose
misuse mistook taken alcohol induced bee-hive excuse.
Claims to be deep dyslexic fog and monster subterfuge.

The hair lacquer past where multiple percussionists drive
like motorbikes round a circular track is the place where it all
begins. Dance dance three-minute teenage angst.

Rebel rebel. Made more money than any rebel should.
Magic inside a bizarre little man with lifts in his shoes
a Jewish wig and many guns. Shot them kept shooting.
Didn't realise, he said. Tried for killing
B-movie Lana Clarkson. Bruised tongue, bullet in the head.
Phil said she did it herself. No Spector dna under her nails.
Evidence hidden. Phil firing lawyers like a magnate.
A jury of twelve selected from a brave three hundred.
After twenty-seven weeks there was a split verdict.
Ten he did it. Two he did not.

To know know know him is to love love love him.

Retrial. He hit me. It felt like a kiss.

Like *Groundhog Day* the hearing rolled again. Wigs
in an endless spin.
Then finally a shot of him with his hand shake shaking. All rise.
Spector undone.

Ifor Ifor at 60

For Ifor Thomas, read on the day in glorious sun, on the top of Pen y Fan, Brecon Beacons, highest peak in south Wales.

Ifor Ifor ap Ifor Ifor.
Ifor of the cardboard box, the smoke,
the toilet seat and half a book.
Ifor, greeny-green bluestone avoider,
WNO Johnny come lately loud-poem chainsaw waver.
Ifor, weather braver cliff jumper pom pounder.
Soap in the cleats of his floozy shoes.
Blues banger tremendous titillator tingly torchbearer
Tôpher beating tool-wielding left fielder
tan ta tip tip trippipip ip aaahhh Trippo
- would have won you twice if they'd let me.
Taff bestrider hot-floored hospital maker
(not us no)
former willy thriller   killer diller
Mr Spock Adrian Henri Lenny Cohen
in some lights resembler.
Waste-water diviner fixer mixer love-spoon rhymer
Curtis client now life's done some flying
check the walls.
The poems glow.
(it's the much younger Gill's birthday too
Sue said I should add this
so I have).
Ifor I salute you.

Our Lady of the Sacred Blood

At the Our Lady of the Sacred Blood
Pumped By The Holy Heart School
for the Fallen, on Bofin, Annie has yet to
change her name to Fionnuala ni Ghiobúin
in order to better her chances
of a glowing Irish job.

She is studying deportment and how
to enter a room so you don't present the
world with your arse (you shut the door
with your hand behind you), how to
descend stairs (sideways as a crab not
directly like a galloping horse), and
how to speak – you don't – you let
the world stay still and not fill it with
foaming chatter.

She is taught by a nun in a wimple
who has explained to her how to sit
with your legs straight and never crossed
and detailed the perils of patent shoes
which in their shiny wonder
could show the world your knickers
and cause grown men to fumble.

In the lesson on how to ride home in
the back of a Morris Traveller when
all the seats are taken and you are forced to
ride on the knee of a kindly uncle she is
told to always place a glossy magazine
in the empty lap in order to hold back
any stirring from his member.

She learns, she does.
The future is now a safe place with
its Irish skies, furnished with
endless cloud, rolling past the Sacred
Blood like saints slowly dancing.

The Seven Wonders

Fore – County West Meath, Ireland

In the night we'd heard the weather arriving like a barbarian hoard. Slashing, chanting, fighting, burning. All day we crossed the bottomless bog seeing fields of furious green and vast sheets of empty water. The forecast had warned that even for the west this was exceptional, the world drowning in the thing that brings it life. The earth emulsifying. At Fore where St Feichin perpetuated his seven wonders – the wood you couldn't burn, the mill that turned without a race, the water that ran uphill, the stone that flew into the sky, the penitent bricked into the Abbey walls, some others I can't now recall but huge things that make you blink, even now – Daf showed us the two pubs, the one with half a garage bolted onto its front and kids toys in baskets for sale where he'd always gone and The Abbey, the real one, smelling of dry rot where he hadn't. Warned against it by his grandfather two generations back when the sectarian reasons were clear although today like many things here they were no longer. Still has never crossed its welcoming door. As we look the rain sets in again like a bursting bombard of tossed grain, puts us back in the car to drive on to where it might stop but never does, to where the land gives out in a emerald flail and the sea itself gets rained on in some sort of storm-lovers orgy. Water, how many kinds of you are there? Fall and foam, floe and flud, flash and flail. Never enough.

Now You Can Again Be Your Father

The cat has a name but
suddenly you can't think of it. In
the wardrobe are 18 pairs of shoes
you do not wear. The poor had none
when you were younger.

Last week couldn't find anyone
who could remember Gary US Bonds.
This week still can't

Time is in the next room
hissing like a cistern
almost spent.

Soon you'll become what you
were always going to,
only culture held you back.
Needed to be something, desperately.
Now you can again be your father.
His jacket when he was sixty fits me now
used to be like a tent.

He couldn't really swim either
said he could.
Breathing ineffectually down
the pool at tai chi speeds
overtaken by toddlers with
floatation devices
and men who had lost limbs.

I sat in the chair he used
still there in the back room
like a megalith
went ahhh.
This only starts when you are
over 50.

Lost:
string driving gloves
jubbly
telegrams
bosoms with points
hard-rind cheese
fishwives
smuts in your eyes

Length of time it takes to open
a shrink wrapped CD:
5 minutes 20 including scissors.
World record is 2 seconds flat.

He stuck to lps. Liked Edmundo Ros.
Told me that if you could get
women to dance then you were half way there
didn't say where that was.

Mambo, samba, things that were in the blood.

Beat

John Tripp 59
B S Johnson 41
Arthur Rimbaud 37
Buddy Holly 29

Kingsley Amis 74
not managed him yet

My father said poems were
things you used when you died
air fresheners for the eternal soul

Basho's was

on a journey, ailing,
my dreams roam about
over a withered moor

He never liked the moors, my father,
but I did

full of space and incessant air

that's me over there
that smudge
big coat no hair
just like my father
slowly mamboing into the future.

Notes

Zen Cymru: Composed as an interactive piece of web poetry. The original is at http://www.peterfinch.co.uk/zen.htm

The Miró Mini Bar: Miro might have been born here in Barcelona or perhaps it was at Montroig nearby. Joan Miró (1893-1983) one of the best painters Catalonia has ever produced.

N Wst Brdg: A commissioned rewrite of Wordsworth's most famous sonnet, made as a text message for the original's two hundredth's anniversary.

Llywelyn Goch ap Meurig Hen At Speed: A translation from the Welsh original made by running past the original text much in the way that motorway drivers pass roadsigns.

Trying To Find Béla Bartók: The composer is buried in the cemetery at Farkasréti Temetö, Budapest. *köszönöm* – Thank you.

Entry of Christ Into Cardiff 2005: Adrian Henri painted his *Entry of Christ into Liverpool* in (1962/1964). It was in homage to James Ensor's painting *The Entry of Christ into Brussels* (1889). There is no such painting yet to celebrate the Welsh capital.

Kerdif: The acrostic section of this poem has been inscribed into the paving in Hayes Place, Cardiff, immediately outside the new central library and the front entrance to John Lewis. It forms part of Jean Bernard Metais' art installation, *Alliance*. In the original version of this piece text was to be projected from the top to the ground by way of a series of high powered gobos. That component of the project was lost in a recessionary cost cut. The original text is included here. How did Cardiff get its name and how was it written down the centuries. Take a look.

The Ballast Bank: This is the original (and slightly longer version) of the text which has now been incorporated into Renn and Thackers' *Blue Light* public artwork at the entrance to the new South Wales Police Headquarters on James Street, Cardiff. This station is built very near where in the early days of Cardiff as a trading port stood a quarter mile bank of ballast, dumped there by arriving ships. The art work puts some of that ballast bank back. The poem delineates the races, language groupings, trades and ideas which flowed in and out of the burgeoning industrial town as it exponentially developed.

Acknowledgements

Some of the poems in this collection, often in earlier versions, were first published in the following anthologies and magazines:

Agenda, The Argoist Online, Around The Globe, The Bare Essential John Tripp – edited by Tony Curtis (Parthian), *Big Bridge, Creative Writing: Theory Beyond Practice* – edited by Nigel Krauth & Tess Brady (Post Pressed, Australia), *Earth Has Not Any Thing to Shew More Fair* – Edited by Peter Oswald, Alice Oswald & Robert Woof (Shakespeare's Globe), *Everybody's Mother* – edited by Linda Coggin & Clare Marlow (Peterloo Poets), *The Literary Review, Long Time Coming – Short Writings From Zimbabwe* ('ama Books) , *The Muse Apprentice Guild, New Welsh Review, P F S Post, The Penniless Press, Planet, Poet Portraits, Poetry 1900-2000* - edited by Meic Stephens (Library of Wales), *Poetry Review, Poetry Wales, Quattrocento, Red Poets, Roundy House, Schriftselle, Short Fuse, Snow Apple, Sport* – edited by Gareth Williams (Library of Wales), *Troubles Swapped For Something Fresh – prose poems*, edited by Rupert Loydell (Salt), *Western Mail, Yellow Crane.*

Thanks are also due to Safle for facilitating the commissions which resulted in the incorporation into public artworks of Kerdif and The Ballast Bank.